CW01646358

The Diving Emergency Handbook

A guide to the identification of and first aid for SCUBA (air) diving injuries

United Kingdom edition

by

John Lippmann
Stan Bugg

and edited by
Dr. Peter Wilmshurst

J.L. Publications **Melbourne**

U.K. Edition published by **J.L. Publications,** PO Box 381, Carnegie, Victoria 3163, Australia in conjunction with **Underwater World Publications,** 55 High St, Teddington, Middlesex TW11 8HA, United Kingdom.

U.K. edition first published in March 1989.

Revised U.K. edition published in March 1993.

Australian, United States, Japanese, German and Italian editions also available.

ISBN 0 946020 18 3

Foreword

Although divers are taught basic first aid, far too frequently, when faced with a real emergency, they cannot remember what action to take. They do nothing or sometimes do the wrong thing. Their friends die or are permanently disabled as a result.

In these situations, what is required is a source of information which can be rapidly consulted to determine what first aid measures should be undertaken and how expert assistance can be obtained. The book needs to be in a form which allows the information to be found quickly and easily and needs to be small and waterproof enough to be taken into a dive boat. **The Diving Emergency Handbook** is such a book.

It was first produced in Australia by John Lippmann and Stan Bugg and has been modified to take into account BS-AC safety procedures.

It is a book for divers, conceived and written by divers. Only the essential information is contained in it. All of the technical small print facts which doctors like to read have been removed and can be found in reference books. However, this does not mean that the book is in any way an amateur effort. It has been checked and approved by medical experts on diving medicine in Australia, the USA, the UK and various other countries.

The present edition is relevant to first aid for British diving accidents. In addition, because British divers often holiday in warmer climates, the first aid of some medical conditions more relevant to exotic places is also included.

Dr. Peter Wilmshurst
Medical Adviser British Sub-Aqua Club

Acknowledgements

We sincerely thank Dr. Peter Wilmshurst for his valuable input and assistance in preparing this United Kingdom edition of our book.

We are also deeply indebted to the following people for editing and providing input into various other editions of the book, some of which are entitled **The DAN Emergency Handbook**. Our thanks go to:

Surgeon Commander Des Gorman (RNZN), Dr. Carl Edmonds, Dr. John Knight, Dr. Janene Mannerheim, John Pennefather, Dr Chris Acott, Professor Peter Bennett, Chris Wachholz, Dr. Richard Moon, Dr. Giles Yancey-Mebane, Dr. Yoshiyuki Gotoh, Professor Dr. Siegfried John, Dr. Max Hahn, Professor Dr. Alessandro Marroni, Dr. John Williamson, Dr. Struan Sutherland, Professor Dr. Albert Buehlmann, Dr. David Parsons, Dr. R. Kelly Hill Jr and Dr. Ian Millar.

The Authors:

John Lippmann

CMAS Three Star SCUBA Diving Instructor
Ex Chief Instructor/Examiner in Oxygen Resuscitation and Instructor/Examiner in Sub Aqua with the Royal Life Saving Society of Australia (Vic).
Author of *Deeper Into Diving*, *The Essentials of Deeper Sport Diving* and *Oxygen First Aid for Divers.*

Stan Bugg

CMAS Three Star Diving Instructor
Instructor/Examiner in Senior Resuscitation and Sub Aqua with the Royal Life Saving Society of Australia (Vic).

Authors' note:

This book is not intended to be a textbook on diving medicine. There is an abundance of excellent books that already cover this field comprehensively. Rather, our book is intended for use at the dive site to assist you in the management of dive related injuries. The plastic pages will allow the book's use in a wet environment, and the alphabetical list of signs and symptoms will, hopefully, guide you quickly towards correct identification and subsequent correct first aid treatment.

Textbooks are important for their detailed information and explanation of the causes of injury, the physiological processes involved and principles behind the treatment procedures. However, our book contains only the essential information required to facilitate rapid first aid. After all, a diver who is suffering the mind-numbing inertia that follows an injury to his buddy will not be interested in a discourse on Boyles law! In these circumstances, this extra information will only serve to delay the victim's treatment.

This book represents many hours of research and consultation with some of the world's foremost authorities on underwater medicine. We are deeply indebted to these experts in underwater medicine who took the time to check our manuscript, and to suggest additions and changes. It is our fervent hope that you will never need to use this book for the purpose for which it was intended.

We realize that women also have diving accidents, but have only used he, him and his instead of he/she and so on for the sake of grammatical ease.

Safe diving

John and Stan

Disclaimer:

The advice outlined in this booklet has been approved, at the time of publication, by some of the world's foremost authorities on Underwater Medicine. The authors stress that treatments may vary with time and should never be used or adopted exclusive of, or in substitution for medical consultation. Users must be aware that this booklet outlines typical rather than definitive signs and symptoms, and therefore first aid administered by untrained personnel in response to apparent signs and symptoms as listed, cannot be guaranteed to succeed.

Contents

How to use this book

1. Look up the sign/symptom in Section A, Symptoms Index,and determine possible ailments.
2. Look up these possible ailments in Section B, Index of Diving Ailments, refer to the appropriate ailments taking note of their causes and other associated signs/symptoms.
3. Determine the most likely ailment.
4. Administer first aid accordingly.

Notes

1. If there is any difficulty in differentiating between possible ailments, then administer first aid as required for the most serious of the likely illnesses.
2. Oxygen should be given whenever possible. (See Page 47)
3. Contact a diving medical specialist without delay. (See inside front cover)
4. Any "illnesses" or symptoms that occur within 36 hours after diving should be regarded as diving-related until proven otherwise.
5. The notes marked "Doctor" are for medical or paramedical personnel only.

Section A:

Index of signs, symptoms and possible causes

NOTE: Many different injuries may cause similar signs and symptoms. The possible causes given here are usually only those that are diving-related. However, in a few cases, some non-diving-related causes are given for consideration. The problems written in *italics* are often not specifically diving-related injuries and are not included in Section 2.

Symptom: Possible Problem:

Aches

Coincident illness, Decompression sickness, Ear barotrauma, Heart attack, Marine animal injury, Pulmonary barotrauma, Salt water aspiration, *Trauma* (eg. from marine animals)

Anxiety

Fright, Nitrogen narcosis, Shock

Apathy

Carbon monoxide toxicity, Decompression sickness, Heat exhaustion, Hypothermia, Salt water aspiration syndrome, Shock

Bite

-small	Fish, Sea snake
-large	Shark, Barracuda, Moray or Conger eel, Boat propellor. *(See Bleeding).*

Bleeding/Blood

-any site	*Trauma*
-blister	Cone shell sting
-from ears	Ear barotrauma, *Head injury*
-from mouth	Dental barotrauma, Ear barotrauma, *Oral trauma*, Pulmonary barotrauma, Sinus barotrauma
-from nose	Ear barotrauma, *Nasal trauma,* Sinus barotrauma, *Head injury*
-in stools	*Coincident illness (eg. Haemorrhoids)*, Decompression sickness
-in sputum	Dental barotrauma, Near drowning,Pulmonary barotrauma, Sinus barotrauma
-in urine	*Coincident illness*, Decompression sickness

Blotchy skin

Decompression sickness, Hypothermia, Shock, Jellyfish sting

Blue lips/Blue skin

Airway obstruction, Carbon monoxide toxicity (rarely), Heart attack, Hypothermia, Marine animal envenomation, Near drowning, Pulmonary barotrauma, Salt water aspiration syndrome

A

Breathing Difficulty

Carbon dioxide toxicity, Carbon monoxide toxicity, Decompression sickness, Marine animal envenomation, Heart attack, Near drowning, Pulmonary barotrauma, Salt water aspiration syndrome

Bruised face

Direct trauma, Facial barotrauma, Rubber allergy (mask)

Burping

Gastrointestinal barotrauma, *Swallowing air*

Chest pain

Decompression sickness, Heart attack, *Muscular sprain,* Near drowning, Pulmonary barotrauma, Salt water aspiration syndrome

Cold/hot flushes

Near drowning, Salt water aspiration syndrome

Cold, clammy skin

Shock

Cold skin

Hypothermia

Convulsions

Arterial gas embolism, Decompression sickness, *Epilepsy, Head injury*, Oxygen toxicity (if breathing oxygen underwater)

Confusion

Arterial gas embolism, Carbon monoxide toxicity, Carotid sinus syndrome, Decompression sickness, *Drugs,* Marine animal injury, Hypothermia, Nitrogen narcosis (if symptom only occurs at depth}

Coughing

Decompression sickness, Near drowning, Pulmonary barotrauma, Salt water aspiration syndrome

Crackly skin (in chest, neck or throat area)

Pulmonary barotrauma

Cramps in stomach

Coincident illness, Decompression sickness, Heat exhaustion, Gastrointestinal barotrauma

Cry, gasping, grunting, on surfacing

Arterial gas embolism, Pulmonary barotrauma

Cyanosis (blueness)

Carbon monoxide toxicity (rarely), Decompression sickness, Heart attack, Hypothermia, Marine animal injury, Near drowning, Pulmonary barotrauma, Salt water aspiration syndrome

Deafness

Decompression sickness, Ear barotrauma, *Impacted wax*

Diarrhoea

Coincident illness, Decompression sickness, Shock

Difficulty swallowing
Cone shell sting, Decompression sickness, Pulmonary barotrauma, Sea snake bite

Dizziness
Alternobaric vertigo, Arterial gas embolism, Carbon dioxide toxicity, Carbon monoxide toxicity, Carotid sinus syndrome, Decompression sickness, Ear barotrauma, Oxygen toxicity, Shock

Drowsiness *(See Apathy)*

Ear pain
Ear barotrauma, "Tight jaw" (ie. biting on mouthpiece too hard/long)

Equalising difficulty
Ear barotrauma, Sinus barotrauma

Fainting *(See inside back cover)*

Flushed appearance
Carbon dioxide toxicity, Carbon monoxide toxicity, Heat exhaustion

Fluid from ear
Ear barotrauma, *Fractured skull*

Froth from mouth
Near drowning, Pulmonary barotrauma, Heart attack

Fullness in throat
Pulmonary barotrauma

Hallucinations
Drug/medication, Nitrogen narcosis (at depth), Oxygen toxicity (if breathing oxygen underwater)

Headache
Arterial gas embolism, Carbon dioxide toxicity, Carbon monoxide toxicity, *Coincident illness*, *Cold water* (no hood), Decompression sickness, Heat exhaustion, *"Tight jaw"* (i.e. biting on mouthpiece too hard, too long), *Tight hood/mask strap*, Sinus barotrauma

Hearing loss *(See Deafness)*

Heart irregularity
Arterial gas embolism, Carotid sinus syndrome, Decompression sickness, decongestant (eg.Psuedoephedrine) or other drugs, Heart attack, Heat exhaustion, Hypothermia, Pulmonary barotrauma, Shock

Heart stops *(See inside back cover)*

Hot flushes
Salt water aspiration syndrome

Inco-ordination
Alcohol, Arterial gas embolism, Decompression sickness, Hypothermia, Marine animal injury, Nitrogen narcosis (if symptom occurs only at depth)

Itching

Decompression sickness; *Drug reaction*; Jellyfish, coral or hydroid sting; *Wetsuit allergy*

Joint pain

Decompression sickness, *Traumatic injury*

Leaning to one side

Arterial gas embolism, Decompression sickness, Ear barotrauma, Pulmonary barotrauma

Light headed

Arterial gas embolism, Decompression sickness, Ear barotrauma, *Hyperventilation*, Nitrogen narcosis (at depth), *Panic*

Lip twitching

Arterial gas embolism, Hypothermia, Oxygen toxicity

Memory loss

Alcohol, Arterial gas embolism, Carbon monoxide toxicity, Decompression sickness, Nitrogen narcosis (if symptom only occurs at depth)

Muscular convulsions

Arterial gas embolism, Carbon dioxide toxicity (severe), Decompression sickness, *Epilepsy*, *Hypoxia*

Muscular paralysis

Arterial gas embolism, Cone shell sting, Decompression sickness, *Head injury,* Sea snake bite

Nausea

Carbon dioxide toxicity, Carbon monoxide toxicity, Decompression sickness, Ear barotrauma, Fish spine injury, Heat exhaustion, Gastrointestinal barotrauma, Sea sickness, Shock, Salt water aspiration syndrome

Numbness

Arterial gas embolism, Cone shell sting, Decompression sickness, Hypothermia, Sea snake bite

Pain

-back &/or neck	Possible causes include Decompression sickness, *muscle strain*, *previous injury*
-ears	Ear barotrauma
-headache	Arterial gas embolism, Carbon dioxide toxicity, Carbon monoxide toxicity, *Cold water , Decompression sickness, Sinus barotrauma*
-joints	Decompression sickness
-stomach	Decompression sickness, Gastrointestinal barotrauma
-teeth	Dental barotrauma, Sinus barotrauma
-urinary	*Coincident illness*, Decompression sickness

Pale skin

Heat exhaustion, Hypothermia, Shock

Paralysis

Arterial gas embolism, Cone shell sting, Decompression sickness, Sea snake bite

Pins and needles

Arterial gas embolism, Decompression sickness, *Hyperventilation*

Pulse

-rapid and weak Shock, Heat Exhaustion

-slow and weak Carotid sinus syndrome, Hypothermia

Puncture marks

Cone shell sting, Fish spine injury, Sea snake bite, *Trauma*

Rapid pulse

Heat exhaustion, Shock

Rash

Decompression sickness, Coral, hydroid or jellyfish sting, Wetsuit allergy

Red eyes

Facial barotrauma (Mask Squeeze)

Red lips

Carbon monoxide toxicity, *Rubber allergy (mouthpiece)*

Ringing ears

Decompression sickness, Ear barotrauma

Shivering

Hypothermia, Salt water aspiration syndrome, Shock

Short of breath

Carbon dioxide toxicity, Carbon monoxide toxicity, Decompression sickness, Heart attack, Marine animal injury, Near drowning, Pulmonary barotrauma, Salt water aspiration syndrome, Shock

Shock *(See Page 39)*

Skin (cold)

Hypothermia, Shock

Slow pulse

Carotid sinus syndrome, Hypothermia

Speech difficulty

Arterial gas embolism, Decompression sickness, Hypothermia, Pulmonary barotrauma

Stiffness in limbs

Decompression sickness, Fish spine injury, Hypothermia

Stinging sensation

Equipment allergy, Jellyfish, coral or hydroid sting

Stomach cramps

Decompression sickness, Heat exhaustion, Gastrointestinal barotrauma

Thirst

Dehydration after diving, Heat exhaustion, Shock

Tightness of face

Facial barotrauma, *Rubber allergy* (mask)

Tingling

Arterial gas embolism, Decompression sickness, *Hyperventilation*

Tooth pain

Dental barotrauma, Sinus barotrauma

Unconsciousness *(See inside back cover)*

Arterial gas embolism, Carbon dioxide toxicity, Carbon monoxide toxicity, Carotid sinus syndrome, *Coincident illness/trauma*, Decompression sickness, Marine animal injury, Nitrogen narcosis, Oxygen toxicity (if breathing oxygen underwater), Pulmonary barotrauma, Shock

Urinary/bowel loss of control to urinate/defecate

Arterial gas embolism, Decompression sickness

Vertigo

Alternobaric vertigo, Arterial gas embolism, Carbon dioxide toxicity, Carbon monoxide toxicity, Decompression sickness, Ear barotrauma, Oxygen toxicity (if breathing oxygen underwater), Shock

Visual disturbances

Arterial gas embolism, Decompression sickness, *Contact lenses*, *Drugs*, Facial barotrauma (rarely), Oxygen toxicity

Voice changes

Arterial gas embolism, Decompression sickness, Pulmonary barotrauma

Vomiting

Carbon monoxide toxicity, *Coincident illness*, Decompression sickness, Ear barotrauma, *Sea sickness*, Shock

Weakness

Arterial gas embolism, Carbon monoxide toxicity, Decompression sickness, Heat exhaustion, Hypothermia, Marine animal injury, Pulmonary barotrauma, Shock

Weals

Decompression sickness, Jellyfish, coral or hydroid sting, *Wetsuit allergy*

Wound, ragged

Marine animal injury, *Trauma*

Section B:

Diving ailments

Arterial Gas Embolism

Cause:

- Holding breath on ascent
- Rapid ascent with inadequate exhalation
- Trapping of air in lungs due to asthma, mucous, water inhalation, laryngeal spasm, cough or cold, smoking and attempts at controlling air escape such as humming on ascent
- Venous gas bubbles entering the arterial system having passed through or bypassed the lungs
  Arterial gas embolism can occur after a normal ascent. Diving with a cough or cold increases the risk of arterial gas embolism. There is an increased incidence after normal ascent in smokers.

Signs and symptoms:

will usually develop within 5-10 minutes of surfacing but occasionally may take longer

Unconsciousness
Headache
Confusion
Speech/visual disturbances
Dizziness
Convulsion
Weakness/Inco-ordination
Numbness/tingling sensation
Paralysis
Death
Symptoms of pulmonary barotrauma may also be present

First aid: must be rapid

- Monitor the consciousness, breathing and pulse and resuscitate if necessary *(See inside back cover)*
- Lay the patient down horizontally, maintain his airway, and ensure that his head is no higher than his chest. **Do not let the patient raise his head.** If the diver is nauseated, vomiting or not fully conscious he should be placed in the recovery (three-quarters prone) position. **If resuscitation is required, the patient should be placed flat on his back.**
- Administer 100% oxygen

- Seek medical aid immediately. Arrange for attending medical personnel to contact a diving medical specialist
- Arrange for transfer to a recompression chamber *(See inside front cover)*
- Give non-alcoholic fluids (eg. water, electrolyte type fluids), **but only if the diver is fully conscious, stable and can drink without raising his head (eg. through a straw)**
- Record details of dive profile, first aid given and diver's response to first aid

Note:

The patient should receive medical treatment even if he appears to return to normal.

Doctor:

Insert an I.V. line with fluids as soon as possible. Crystalloids should be used in preference to water. *Adjunctive therapy should be discussed with the Hyperbaric Centre*. Entonox should never be given.

Alternobaric Vertigo

Cause:

Uneven pressure stimulation of the balance mechanism in the ear due to:

- Eustachian tube blockage
- Unequal middle ear pressures

Signs and symptoms:

Vertigo
Nausea

First aid:

- Stop the descent/ascent
- Equalise adequately
- Ascend slowly

Bleeding (severe)

Signs and symptoms:

Extensive, ragged wounds/lacerations
Severe bleeding
Shock
Unconsciousness
Death (can occur within minutes)

First aid: must be rapid

- Apply direct pressure to the wound (use a pressure pad, packing or bandage).
- If direct pressure fails, use indirect pressure (pressure point or tourniquet) *(See Note 1)*
- Elevate the wound
- Apply Artificial Ventilation/Chest Compression as required *(See inside back cover)*
- Pressure dressing if necessary *(See Note 1)*
- Treat for shock *(See Page 39)*
- Avoid moving the patient unnecessarily *(See Note 2)*
- Send for an ambulance

Note 1:

A tourniquet should only be used as a last resort and, if used, must be released to allow some blood flow every 20 minutes, and only reapplied if necessary to prevent significant bleeding.

Note 2:

If transporting the injured diver is unavoidable, do so with the patient lying down, with his legs elevated if possible. *The patient must be handled gently to minimise shock.*

Carbon Dioxide Toxicity

Cause:

Inadequate ventilation due to:

- Skip breathing
- Faulty regulator
- Tight wetsuit
- Exertion
- Deep diving
- Contamination of the air supply (rare)

Signs and symptoms:

Rapid breathing
Headache
Dizziness
Flushed appearance
Nausea
Vomiting
Confusion
Muscular convulsions (with contaminated air supply)
Unconsciousness (can occur with exertion at depth or contaminated air supply)

First aid:

- Return to surface
- Cease movement
- Breathe normally
- Oxygen
- Expect rapid improvement
- Rescue and resuscitation as appropriate in a very severe case

Carbon Monoxide Toxicity

Cause:

Contaminated air supply due to:

- Faulty compressor
- Exhaust fumes entering compressor air inlet (Hookah divers beware of wind/tide changes!)

Signs and symptoms:

Headache
Irritability, Confusion, Memory loss, Apathy, Drowsiness
Dizziness
Nausea
Vomiting
Shortness of breath
Blueness (occasionally)
Flushed appearance (occasionally)
Weak pulse
Unconsciousness
Death (cherry-red lips and fingernail beds may sometimes be visible)

First aid:

- Remove from the source
- Monitor the consciousness, breathing and pulse and resuscitate if necessary *(See inside back cover)*
- Administer 100% oxygen
- Medical aid
- Hospital
- Hyperbaric oxygen treatment may be needed

Note:

It is possible to have carbon monoxide toxicity without any obvious signs or symptoms.

Carotid Sinus Syndrome

Cause:

Tight-fitting wetsuit top or dry suit neck seal exerting excess pressure on the neck. (May follow a rapid ascent in a drysuit, especially after a blowup with a large bubble of air collecting under the neck seal, which fails to give. So this syndrome may be combined with pulmonary barotrauma.)

Signs and symptoms:

Slow pulse
Confusion, Disorientation
Fainting
Nausea

First aid:

- Loosen or remove the wetsuit top or dry suit neck seal

Cone Shell Sting

Signs and symptoms:

Sometimes pain
Wound may become red and swollen (looks like blood blister)
Numbness, Weakness, Muscular paralysis
Breathing stops
Heart stops

First aid:

- Monitor airway, breathing and circulation and resuscitate if necessary *(See inside back cover)*
- Pressure-Immobilisation *(See Page 43)*
- Monitor the patient and keep him still, quiet and reassured
- Identify the cone
- Seek medical aid

Note:

The pressure bandage must not occlude the circulation (the fingers/toes beyond the bandage should remain pink and with normal sensation). The bandage should be left in place until proper medical support is available.

Decompression Sickness

Decompression sickness is caused by the presence of nitrogen bubbles in our bodies. It often occurs when decompression tables have been exceeded but **can and does occur even on dives that are well within the no-stop limits of tables, and on dives conducted in accord with any of the various dive computers.**

The following predisposing factors will increase a diver's likelihood of getting decompression sickness even if the tables/computers are followed correctly.

- Repetitive diving (especially multi-day, repetitive diving)
- Deeper diving (i.e. over about 24 m)
- Rapid or multiple ascents
- Exercise before, during or after the dive
- Flying after diving
- Dehydration
- Obesity
- Fatigue, Lack of fitness, Illness, Previous injury, Presence of a patent foramen ovale
- Ingestion of alcohol or various drugs or medications before the dive
- Being cold
- Age - risk appears to increase with age
- Carbon dioxide excess
- Decompression stop diving
- Stress

Note:

If symptoms similar to those of decompression sickness are present after diving, never exclude decompression sickness because of what may appear to be a safe dive according to the tables or computer.

Signs and symptoms:

Although these usually occur within six hours of diving they may develop 24 to 48 hours after the dive, or even later if there is altitude exposure after prolonged diving. **Frequent signs/symptoms of decompression sickness are malaise (feeling unwell) and extreme fatigue.**

Although the symptoms of decompression sickness often disappear they may have serious implications, especially if inappropriately treated.

Common:

Chest, torso or back pain
Dizziness
Extreme fatigue
Headaches
Malaise
Numbness
Pain/discomfort at or near a joint
Tingling sensations
Weakness

Other:

Blood in stools
Blotchy skin
Confusion
Convulsions
Coughing
Difficulty passing urine
Hearing loss
Inco-ordination
Itch
Loss of balance
Loss of bladder/bowel control
Nausea
Paralysis
Rash
Ringing in ears
Shortness of breath
Unconsciousness
Visual disturbances

First aid:

- Monitor consciousness, breathing and pulse and resuscitate if necessary *(See inside back cover)*
- Lay the patient down and maintain his airway.
- Administer 100% oxygen
- Seek medical aid. Arrange for the attending medical personnel to contact a diving medical specialist.
- Arrange transfer to a recompression chamber *(See inside front cover)*
- A conscious and stable patient may drink small quantities of non-alcoholic fluids (eg. water, isotonic/electrolyte fluids) *(See Note)*
- Record details of dive profile and previous dives
- Record details of first aid given and patient's response to first aid

Note:

I.V. fluids are preferable. Oral fluids are given only if the patient is conscious, stable and is *not* suffering from stomach pain, urinary retention or paralysis *unless* a urinary catheter is used. Record amount and type of fluid given. Record urinary output and check for bladder distension. *If the bladder becomes distended give no more fluid until a urinary catheter is inserted.*

Doctor:

Insert an I.V. line of normal saline or Ringers Lactate as soon as possible. *Adjunctive therapy should be discussed with the Hyperbaric Centre.* Entonox should never be given.

Warning:

Do not return patient to the water

Dental Barotrauma

Cause:

Air trapped in a cavity beneath a filling

Signs and symptoms:

Tooth pain
Bleeding
Broken tooth

First aid:

- Analgesics as directed
- Arrange dental repair

Note:

Pain in the upper teeth is more commonly a symptom of sinus barotrauma

Ear Barotraumas

Middle ear barotrauma

Caused on descent by:

Inadequate equalisation due to:

- Poor equalising technique
- Diving with a cold, hayfever or flu or obstructed eustachian tube(s)
- Rapid descent

Caused on ascent by:

- Swelling of the middle ear lining due to inadequate equalisation on descent
- Rapid ascent
- Decongestants wearing off underwater

Signs and symptoms:

Fullness in ear
Discomfort
Ear pain during the dive
Hearing loss
Ruptured ear drum
Vertigo during or shortly after the dive
Nausea, Vomiting
Ringing *(See inner ear barotrauma)*
Blood from nose, mouth or ear

First aid:

- Ascend slowly
- Analgesics as directed
- Decongestants
- Do not equalise forcefully
- Consult a diving doctor

Note:

If dizziness, hearing loss or ringing continue, consult a diving doctor immediately

External ear barotrauma

Caused on descent by:

- Tight hood
- Blocked outer ear canal due to wax or exostoses
- Mask strap over ear

Signs and symptoms: (usually mild)

Pain in ear, not relieved by equalisation
Discharge/bleeding from ears
Other symptoms similar to those of middle ear barotrauma may occur if ear drum ruptures

First aid:

- Same as for middle ear barotrauma

Inner ear barotrauma

Cause:

- Forceful equalisation of ears
- Severe middle ear barotrauma

Signs and symptoms:

Vertigo
Nausea, Vomiting
Ringing
Hearing loss
These symptoms normally persist for more than 15-20 minutes after the dive

First aid:

- Sit down and keep still and quiet
- Avoid exertion, coughing, sneezing, bending over and further attempts to equalise the ears
- **Consult diving doctor or ear, nose and throat specialist immediately**

Facial Barotrauma

Cause:

Failure to equalise the pressure inside the mask with the ambient pressure.

Signs and symptoms:

Tightness on face
Red/bruised face
Red eyes
Change in vision (rarely)

First aid:

- Cease diving until the injury has healed
- If change in vision occurs see a doctor to check for bleeding

Fish Spine Injuries

(including injuries from the Crown of Thorns starfish and from sea urchins)

Cause:

Puncture from the spines of spine-bearing fish (eg. Weeverfish in U.K., Scorpion, Stonefish or Stingrays in tropics)

Signs and symptoms:

Puncture wound/laceration
Immediate pain (acute if venomous)
Some bleeding
Nausea, Vomiting
Shock
Death (occasionally)

First aid:

- Control any severe bleeding, if present *(See Page 16)*
- Remove the spine, if present
- Immerse the wound in hot, but not scalding, fresh water. (Test the water temperature yourself before immersing the patient's wound). Leave immersed for 30-90 minutes for pain relief. This may be repeated if pain recurs. (Outboard engine cooling water can be used if necessary)
- Treat for shock *(See Page 39)*
- Analgesics as directed
- Clean the wound by scrubbing it with soap and fresh water then rinse it thoroughly with fresh water. Apply local antiseptics
- Medical advice

Doctor:

- Injection of local anaesthetic (without adrenalin) gives relief and allows better cleaning
- Antivenom is available for Stonefish stings
- Tetanus toxoid if indicated
- Secondary infection is common
- Look carefully for any part of spine still in the wound. X-ray of injury site for retained spine fragments may be advisable

Gastrointestinal Barotrauma

Cause:

Gas may enter the stomach due to:

- Swallowing air
- Equalising ears when swimming head down
- Gas produced from certain foods and drinks

This gas will expand on ascent and may cause a barotrauma or distension

Signs and symptoms:

Stomach pain/cramps
Burping
Flatulence
Sometimes difficulty breathing

First aid:

- Stop the ascent
- Release the gas
- Continue ascent when comfortable

Heart Attack

Predisposing factors:

These include: Male gender, increased age, history of heart disease, family history of heart disease, high blood pressure, over exertion, obesity, diabetes, smoking, use of certain drugs/medications before diving.

Signs and symptoms:

Central chest pain which may radiate to the arms and up to the jaw
Indigestion, nausea
Pallor, sweating
Anxiety
Shortness of breath
Heart irregularities (eg. palpitations)
Dizziness
Unconsciousness
No breathing
No pulse
Cyanosis (blueness)
Fixed dilated pupils

First aid:

Unconscious patient

See inside back cover

Conscious patient

- Patient may prefer to sit up if short of breath
- Give oxygen
- Monitor the airway, breathing and pulse
- Immediate medical assistance

Heat Exhaustion
Heat Stroke

Cause:

- Exposure to high temperatures
- Wearing a wetsuit for extended periods before or after diving in hot weather

Signs and symptoms:

Heat Exhaustion:

Headaches, Dizziness, Nausea
Rapid, weak pulse
Excessive sweating
Muscle cramps
Headache
Pale skin
Weakness
Faintness
Body temperature is normal

Heat Stroke:

Sweating stops
Hot, red, dry skin
Unconsciousness
Pulse is rapid, full and strong
Body temperature is high
(Rectal temperature 40°C or more)

First aid:

Heat Exhaustion:

- Transfer the patient to cool surroundings
- Remove the patient's excess clothing
- Lay the patient down and raise his legs slightly
- Sponge the patient with cool water
- Give the patient sips of water (unless patient is very nauseated)

Heat Stroke:

- Heat stroke is a medical emergency. **Arrange medical assistance immediately**
- Transfer the patient to cool surroundings
- Remove the patient's excess clothing
- Lay the patient down
- Monitor the airway, breathing and pulse. If patient is unconscious *see inside back cover*
- Cool the patient by sponging him with cold water or wrapping him in cool, wet sheets/towels

Hypothermia

Cause:

Cooling of the body core temperature.

Signs and symptoms:

Mild:

Numbness
Blotchy skin
Pallor, blueness of extremities
Shivering

Severe:

Uncontrollable shivering
Inco-ordination
Confusion, Weakness, Apathy, Irritability, Slurred speech, Memory impairment
Muscle rigidity
No shivering in spite of being very cold
Unconsciousness
Dilated, fixed pupils (not necessarily a sign of irreversible brain damage)
No response to pain, Absent reflexes
Difficulty in detecting respiration and pulse
Heart irregularities
Death

First aid:

Must be rapid in order to prevent further heat loss

Mild:

- If adequate dry coverings are available, remove the patient's wetsuit and replace it with dry coverings. If this is impractical (such as when in a small boat), leave the casualty in his wetsuit and dry the surface of the suit as much as possible. Ensure the head and neck are protected
- Insulate the patient from the cold, rain and wind. Placing the patient in waterproof clothing or a large plastic exposure bag/sheet

will keep the wind off and minimise chilling through evaporation. Cover with blankets, if available

- Warm drinks *(See Note 1)*

Severe:

- **Arrange medical assistance immediately**
- Handle the patient very gently, do not actively rewarm in the field
- Carefully assess the presence or absence of pulse and breathing. (Take up to one minute since both may be very weak and slow). If the wetsuit needs to be removed, it may be necessary to carefully cut it off, especially the hood and neck section
- If resuscitation is required *read Note 2 below then see inside back cover*
- If adequate dry coverings are available, very carefully remove the patient's wetsuit and replace it with dry coverings. If this is impractical, leave the casualty in his wetsuit and dry the surface of the wetsuit as much as possible
- Insulate the patient from the elements (as described previously). A huddle of bodies provides a good substitute if adequate other insulation is not available.
- Monitor the airway, breathing and pulse
- Give fluids depending on the patient's condition *(See Note 1)*
- Keep the diver lying down (as he rewarms and the blood vessels dilate, he may become shocked)
- The patient must go to hospital for observation, even if apparently fully recovered

Note 1 (Re fluids):

a. No alcohol, coffee or other high caffeine sources
b. Warm fluids can be given only after uncontrollable shivering stops,the victim has a clear level of consciousness, appears stable and has the ability to swallow.

Note 2 (Re resuscitation):

Some casualties have made successful recoveries after resuscitation following prolonged periods of immersion, without breathing, especially in cold waters (ie. below about 21°C). **If resuscitation is commenced it should not be stopped until the body core temperature has returned to more than 36°C and then only on the direction of a doctor**.

Near Drowning

Cause:

Inhalation of fluids

Signs and symptoms:

Coughing
Shortness of breath
Chest pain
Shock
Blue lips and tongue
Frothy sputum
Unconsciousness
Clenched teeth
Irregular or no breathing
Weak or absent pulse

First aid:

- Clear mouth and ventilate at first opportunity if breathing is absent
- Remove diver from water
- Establish and maintain a clear airway

If patient unconscious:

Read Note below then see inside back cover

If patient conscious:

- Administer 100% oxygen
- Treat for shock
- Send for an ambulance
- Patient must go to hospital for observation

Note:

Patients have been successfully resuscitated after being immersed, without breathing, for prolonged periods; especially in cold water (ie. below about 21°C). If resuscitation is required, continue until relieved by medical aid.

Nitrogen Narcosis

Cause:

When breathed under pressure nitrogen has an intoxicating effect. The effect will be experienced by all divers breathing air at depths in excess of 30m, although some will notice the effect at shallower depths. It increases with depth but is readily reversed on ascent. Certain factors increase the likelihood of a diver suffering from narcosis. Some of these factors are:

- Anxiety, apprehension or inexperience
- Recent intake of alcohol or of certain drugs or medications (eg. sedatives)
- Fatigue
- Heavy work
- Carbon dioxide excess
- Rapid descent
- Poor visibility
- Cold water

Signs and symptoms:

Impairment of reasoning, judgement, memory, concentration, attention
Sense of well-being, light-headedness
Anxiety
Loss of co-ordination, judgement, skill
Hallucinations, unconsciousness, death (at extreme depths)

First aid:

- Protect the diver from injury until ascent is sufficient to eliminate the narcosis

Note:

If the symptoms persist after the ascent to the surface, the cause is something other than narcosis.

Oxygen Toxicity (CNS)

Cause:

When oxygen is breathed at partial pressures usually (but not always) greater than 1.6 ATA, it produces toxicity rapidly and affects the central nervous system (CNS). The likelihood of CNS oxygen toxicity increases with oxygen partial pressure, exposure time, exercise, cold, anxiety and increasing carbon dioxide levels in the blood.

Divers at risk of CNS oxygen toxicity include those who dive on air to depths approaching and exceeding 66 m, those who dive using gas mixtures with an increased percentage of oxygen, and those who use oxygen during decompression (as well as those who require recompression for decompression sickness, arterial gas embolism or carbon monoxide toxicity).

Signs and symptoms:

(occur whilst underwater or shortly after surfacing)

Dizziness
Nausea
Twitching of muscles, particularly of face
Difficulty in concentration
Disorientation
Lightheadedness
Visual abnormalities
Unconsciousness
Convulsion

First Aid

- Bring casualty to surface (if a convulsion is occurring underwater, wait until it ceases before ascending) and remove from water
- Monitor the airway, breathing and pulse and resuscitate if necessary *(See inside back cover)*

Note:

When oxygen is breathed for long periods at partial pressures greater than about 0.6 ATA, symptoms such as coughing, wheezing, shortness of breath and pain behind the breastbone may result. It does not generally threaten the sport diver unless he requires recompression, in which case he is carefully monitored for signs of toxicity and the oxygen level is reduced if necessary.

Pulmonary Barotrauma

Cause:

- Holding breath on ascent
- Rapid ascent ascent with inadequate exhalation
- Trapping of air in lungs due to asthma, smoking, mucous, water inhalation, laryngeal spasm, cough or cold, or attempts at controlling air escape such as humming on ascent

Signs and symptoms:

Shortness of breath
Chest pain
Coughing (sometimes bloody sputum)
Cyanosis (blueness)
Shock
Heart irregularities
Heart attack
Crackly skin
Voice changes
Fullness in throat
Difficulty swallowing
Lean to affected side
Poor chest movement of affected side
Deviated windpipe
Symptoms of arterial gas embolism may also be present

First aid:

- Monitor consciousness, breathing and pulse and resuscitate if necessary *(See inside back cover)*
- Lay the patient down and maintain his airway *(See Note 1)*
- Administer 100% oxygen
- Seek medical aid immediately. Arrange for attending medical personnel to contact a diving medical specialist
- Arrange for transfer to a recompression chamber. *(See inside front cover)*

(Continued over page ...)

- Give non-alcoholic fluids (e.g. water, electrolyte type fluids), **but only if the patient is fully conscious and appears to be stable**
- Record details of dive profile, first aid given and patient's response to first aid

Note 1:

If symptoms of arterial gas embolism are present, ensure that the diver's head is no higher than his chest and do not let the patient raise his head. If the diver is nauseated, vomiting or not fully conscious he should be placed in the recovery (three-quarters prone) position. If resuscitation is required, place the diver flat on his back.

Note 2:

The patient should receive medical treatment even if he appears to return to normal.

Doctor:

- Insert an intravenous line with fluids as soon as possible
- Insert a chest drain for tension pneumothorax if indicated
- Adjunctive therapy should be discussed with the Hyperbaric Centre
- Entonox should not be given

Salt Water Aspiration Syndrome

Cause:

Inhalation of a fine mist of water vapour due to:

- Faulty regulator
- Inadequate mouthpiece seal
- Inadequate purging of regulator or snorkel

Signs and symptoms:

Immediate cough
Possibly a latent period then:
Shortness of breath
Chest pain
Coughing
Cyanosis (blueness)
Uncontrollable shivering
Hot and cold flushes/fever
Rapid pulse
Nausea, Vomiting
Aches
Apathy

First aid:

- Administer 100% oxygen (should cause rapid improvement)
- Keep warm
- Give analgesics as directed
- Discourage unnecessary movement
- Diving medical advice
- Patient may need to go to hospital for observation

Note:

Symptoms of salt water aspiration syndrome may be similar to those of pulmonary barotrauma. If in doubt, treat as the latter.

Sea Snake Bite

Signs and symptoms:

Puncture marks
Stiffness in limbs
Aching
Dark brown urine
Muscular contractions, Weakness
Numbness
Difficulty breathing
Blueness of lips and tongue
Muscular paralysis
Breathing stops
Heart stops

First aid:

- Apply Artificial Ventilation/Chest Compression as required *(See inside back cover)*
- Pressure-Immobilisation *(See Page 43)*
- Keep the patient still, quiet and reassured
- Monitor the airway, breathing, circulation
- Medical aid

Note:

The pressure bandage must not occlude the circulation (the fingers/toes beyond the bandage should remain pink and with normal sensation). The bandage should be left in place until proper medical support is available.

Shock

Cause:

Reduction in effective circulation due to decompression sickness, haemorrhage, injury, infection, illness, burns, dehydration, vomiting, diarrhoea, fright, anxiety or emotional distress. *May be associated with any other injury, illness or emotional upset.*

Signs and symptoms:

Cold, clammy, pale skin
Rapid, weak pulse
Rapid, shallow breathing
Weakness, Collapse
Thirst
Nausea, Vomiting
Confusion, Anxiety
Unconsciousness, Death

First aid:

- Monitor the airway, breathing, circulation and resuscitate if necessary *(See inside back cover)*
- Act to prevent further shock. **Stop any severe (arterial) bleeding**
- Place the patient in a flat position or with head down and legs elevated. **Unconscious patients must be placed in the recovery position to avoid aspiration of vomitus and to maintain an adequate airway**
- Administer oxygen
- Keep the patient still, quiet and reassured
- Protect from the environment
- Medical advice
- Nothing by mouth
- No direct heat

Sinus Barotrauma

Cause:

Equalisation problems due to nasal congestion or anatomical deformity.

Signs and symptoms:

Facial pain or headache which can occur in the forehead, behind the eyes, in the cheeks or upper teeth. The pain increases with depth and then ceases. Can also occur on ascent.
Blood/mucous from the nose
Headache

First aid:

- Analgesics as directed
- Decongestants. (An effective decongestant is saline - 1.5ml (1/4 tsp) salt in 250ml (1 cup) of water at body temperature. Snuff it up the nose, one nostril at a time, and then spit it out. Can be repeated as required)
- Medical advice

Stings from Jellyfish, Corals, Hydroids and Anemones

Signs and symptoms:

Stinging sensation, acute local pain
Red rash, raised weals
Lymph gland pain (usually later)
Shock
Difficulty breathing
Unconsciousness
Death

First aid:

- Monitor airway, breathing and pulse and resuscitate if necessary. *(See inside back cover)*
- Pour **vinegar** over the wound (except for stings from the Portugeuse Man O'War (Physalia) or from the Hair Jellyfish (Cyanea))
- Remove any adherent tentacles (do not use bare hands)
- Cooling agent (eg. ice packs) may provide some pain relief
- Treat for shock *(See Page 39)*
- Immediate medical aid if:
  - stung by Box Jellyfish (Chironex), unless trivial (antivenom is available for Chironex)
  - severe pain and/or difficulty breathing
  - scarring possible

Note (Re coral cuts):

Coral cuts can cause serious secondary infections if adequate first aid is not given. Thoroughly clean the wound using fresh water (not sea water) as soon as possible. Use an antiseptic lotion with a soft brush and remove all foreign material. Apply a local antibiotic powder or ointment, or "Betadine" (iodine paint) if an antibiotic is not available. Follow-up medical care is recommended for coral cuts.

Note (Re Box Jellyfish):

Pressure-Immobilisation may be helpful with a Chironex sting but should only be applied after dousing the tentacles with vinegar and removing them.

Section C:

Appendices

Pressure-immobilisation technique

Courtesy of Dr. Struan Sutherland

1. Immediately apply a broad firm bandage around the limb to cover the bitten area as tightly as one would bind a sprained ankle. As much of the limb should be bound up as possible. Crepe bandages or any flexible material can be used.
2. Keeping the limb as still as possible, bind some type of splint to it – any rigid object will do.
3. Leave bandages and splint intact until medical care is reached.

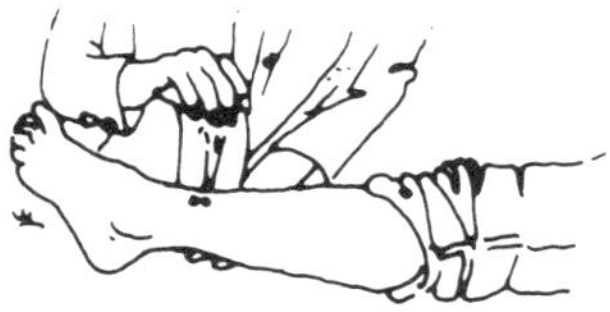

1. Apply a broad firm bandage over the bite as soon as possible. Keep the bitten area still.

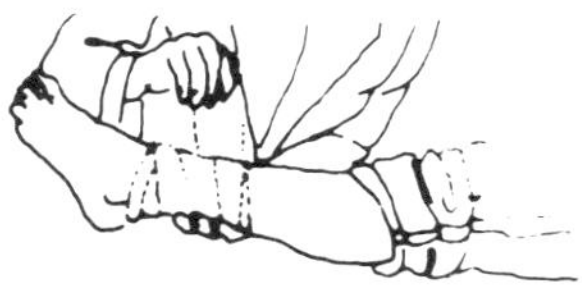

2. The bandage should be as tight as you would apply to a sprained ankle.

3. Extend the bandages as high as possible.

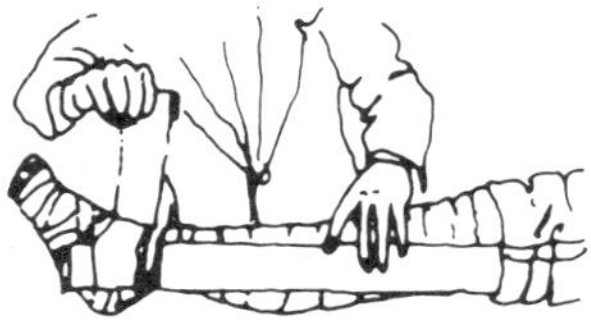

4. Apply a splint to the limb.

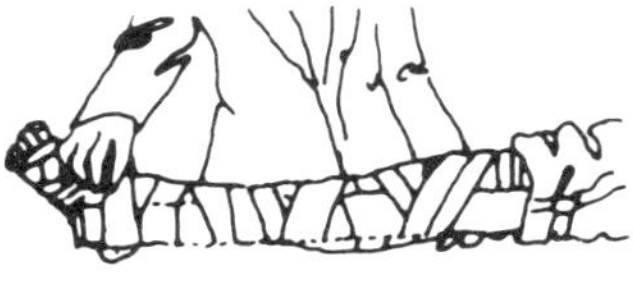

5. Bind it firmly to as much of the limb as possible.

Bites on the hand or forearm.

1. Bind to elbow with bandages.
2. Use splint to elbow.
3. Use sling.

Caution:

The pressure bandage must not occlude the circulation (the fingers/toes beyond the bandage should remain pink and with normal sensation). The bandage should be left in place until proper medical support is available.

Lost Diver Procedure

In the event of a diver(s) not surfacing when expected:

- Assess the degree of urgency. Consider time overdue, planned dive profile (i.e. maximum depth, total dive time) and possible decompression and air status
- Question the buddy, if available, to determine:
  - any obvious problem
  - where and when missing diver was last seen, what he was doing and the direction in which he was swimming
  - maximum depth reached
  - last known air contents and likely air consumption
  - experience and condition of the missing diver
  - diver's likely action in the event of separation and/or emergency
  - where buddy surfaced relative to separation point
- Re-assess degree of urgency in light of information gathered
- Buoy the area where the diver was last seen
- Place a lookout at the highest possible vantage point. Scan the surface/shoreline for divers and bubbles
- Check that diver has not boarded neighbouring boats, if present
- Consider whether it is necessary to conduct an underwater search, a surface search, or both
- If it appears a search is necessary, recall all divers. If an underwater search is to be conducted, prepare the standby divers. Determine who is able to participate in a search, if necessary, without compromising their safety.
- If bubbles are visible send in a pair of standby divers to investigate
- Phone or radio for help (can use the PANPAN urgency call on the radio). Notify Coast Guard
- Utilise any available boats and divers and prepare an appropriate search
- Consider current movement/change. Concentrate search down-current from where diver was last seen but also check up-current
- Do not endanger search divers

Dive Tables and Computers

The fact that many cases of decompression sickness occur following the correct use of dive tables or dive computers prompts us to urge caution when planning any dive, even if well within the No-Stop Limits.

There is no such thing as a completely safe dive table or computer, since no table or computer allows for the individual variation of divers. Because a diver's predisposition to decompression sickness varies with health, fitness, exercise, level of hydration, cold, and many other factors, what may have been a safe dive on one day could be hazardous on another.

Risk of decompression sickness increases when repetitive dives or deeper dives (i.e. over about 24m) are undertaken. Dives requiring a mandatory decompression stop may also be more hazardous, partly due to the difficulty of doing the stop correctly. Accordingly, it is recommended that deeper and/or decompression stop dives be avoided where possible, and that repetitive dive schedules be calculated conservatively; especially multi-day, repetitive dives.

Rapid or multiple ascents substantially increase a diver's chance of developing decompression sickness. Consequently, divers are urged to train themselves in ascent technique and never to exceed 15m/minute when shallower than about 30 m. Many experts believe that an ascent rate of about 10m/minute is desirable when ascending from depths of around 30m or shallower. The BS-AC '88 Tables require an ascent rate of 6m/minute during the final 6m of ascent.

Divers are advised to go to the maximum depth early in the dive and then progressively and slowly move shallower, ending the dive with a safety stop of at least 3 minutes at 5-6m. This is especially important after a deeper dive or a repetitive dive.

Repetitive dives should become progressively shallower and surface intervals should be maximised. When multi-day diving is conducted for several consecutive days (such as on diving holidays), it is wise to do no more than three dives each day, and to refrain from diving on the 3rd or 4th day.

Flying After Diving

Flying (or otherwise ascending) to a higher altitude after having dived can predispose a diver to decompression sickness unless there has been sufficient surface interval to allow excess gas to diffuse from the body. If insufficient time has been allowed and the ambient pressure is reduced, gas bubbles may form, or existing asymptomatic bubbles may increase in size and cause symptoms of decompression sickness.

We can never be sure exactly when it becomes "safe to fly" after a dive since it will depend on the degree of bubble formation and for how long it persists. There is a gradual reduction in risk with time. It may generally be safe to fly a few hours after a short, single dive. However, after a long dive, or a series of repetitive dives, substantially longer surface intervals may be required, especially after several days of repetitive diving.

Many authorities recommend that, as a general rule, a diver should wait at least 24 hours before flying after an air dive. Sometimes this may be overly conservative, while on other occasions it may not prove to be conservative enough.

The following recommendations accompany the BS-AC '88 Tables:

Flying in a pressurised aircraft is not permissible until the Surface Interval Table indicates that the diver has reached Current Tissue Code B. Before flying in an unpressurised aircraft the diver must reach Current Tissue Code A.

In the case of a pressurised aircraft, the interval required before flying is between 0 to 4 hours, depending on the Surfacing Code after the last dive. Intervals of 10 to 16 hours are required before flying in an unpressurised aircraft.

Note 1:

If a diver has had symptoms of decompression sickness and has not received full recompression treatment, flying can be risky even more than a week after the dive.

Note 2 (Flying before diving):

After a long flight, one is often jet-lagged and dehydrated. Since a diver who dives in this condition is predisposed to decompression sickness, it is advisable not to dive until feeling fully recovered from the flight.

Omitted or Interrupted Decompression

If a diver surfaces from a dive without having completed the required decompression, bubbles might have formed, or might begin to form in his blood or body tissues. Eventually, decompression sickness might ensue. The diver should adopt the following procedure:

- Stay on land. **Do not re-descend**
- Remain at rest
- Breathe 100% oxygen
- Drink non-alcoholic fluids *(See Note on Page 21)*
- Do not dive again for at least 24 hours and then only if no signs/symptoms of decompression sickness had developed

If symptoms occur, the full first aid procedure for decompression sickness must be adopted ***(See Page 21).***

Oxygen First Aid

Breathing elevated concentrations of oxygen is beneficial in the treatment of many diving ailments. Oxygen breathing will increase the oxygenation of any hypoxic body tissues and also help to flush out any dissolved nitrogen and nitrogen present in bubbles. The concentration of inspired oxygen should be as near to 100% as can be reached in order to achieve maximum benefit. 100% oxygen is used because it does not contain any nitrogen or other inert gas.

All dive clubs and dive operators should have suitable oxygen equipment available at the dive site and ensure that their members/staff are adequately trained, and appropriately qualified, to use it. Ideally, all divers should have access to oxygen should it be needed after a dive. *Oxygen breathing should be commenced as soon as possible after a diving accident to gain the maximum benefit. If only a limited supply of oxygen is available, it should be given in heavy concentrations from the time the accident is recognised, until the supply of oxygen is exhausted.* Enough oxygen must be provided for any anticipated transport time between the dive site and the nearest hospital.

There is an array of delivery devices designed for giving oxygen to conscious and/or unconscious patients. However, very little oxygen equipment has been designed specifically for diving accidents. To maximise the benefits of oxygen first aid in diving accidents, 100% oxygen must be delivered. To achieve this a demand delivery system must be used. However, constant flow systems are often used. These are uneconomical for oxygen useage since high flow rates are required to achieve high oxygen concentrations.

A demand system with a tight-sealing oro-nasal mask (covers mouth and nose) is capable of delivering 100% oxygen to both the conscious and unconscious (breathing) victim. A non-breathing diver can be ventilated with relative ease and safety using a pocket-style mask attached to an oxygen outlet with a flow rate of 10 to 15 lpm.

Most equipment used for oxygen resuscitation is capable of delivering high pressure oxygen, and, although it can be extremely effective in trained, skilled hands, it may be ineffectual and potentially hazardous if used incorrectly. Therefore, it must not be used by those untrained in its use.

All divers are strongly advised to undergo training in oxygen administration, and should be thoroughly familiar with any oxygen equipment that they might use. The BS-AC Oxygen Administration Course has been developed to provide divers with this necessary information and instruction.

Some Rules for Using Oxygen

The breathing of oxygen is a first aid measure and must never be substituted for the recompression required in cases of decompression sickness or arterial gas embolism, regardless of the response.

When administering oxygen :

- Position the injured diver appropriately
- Ensure area is well ventilated and that there is nothing burning in the immediate vicinity (including cigarettes)
- Ensure your hands and the equipment are free from oil or grease
- Commence oxygen administration as soon as possible
- Carefully record the periods of oxygen breathing
- Carefully record the patient's response to oxygen
- Continue oxygen provision until the supply is depleted. Interrupt temporarily if the diver vomits, regurgitates, during a seizure or if the diver has difficuilty breathing from the equipment. Recommence oxygen provision as soon as possible
- Divers should normally only administer oxygen to other divers suffering from a diving-related problem

Five Minute Neuro Exam

(Reprinted with permission from the DAN 1991 Underwater Diving Accident Manual)

Examination of a victim's central nervous system soon after an accident may provide valuable information to the doctor responsible for treatment. The Five Minute Neuro Exam is easily learned and performed by individuals with no medical experience at all. It should be practiced on normal divers to achieve proficiency.

The examination can be done step-by-step while reading from this manual. Perform the following steps in order, and record the time and results.

Any test that requires the diver to raise his head above his chest should not be performed on a diver suspected of suffering from arterial gas embolism.

1. Orientation

Does the diver know name and age?
Does the diver know the present location?
Does the diver know what time, day, year it is?

Even though a diver appears alert, the answers to these questions may reveal confusion. Do not omit them!

2. Eyes

Have the diver count the number of fingers you display using two or three different numbers. Check eack eye separately and then together. Have the diver identify a distant object.

Tell the diver to hold the head still, or you gently hold it still, while placing your other hand about 45cm in front of the face. Ask the diver to follow your hand. Now move your hand up and down, then side to side. The diver's eyes should follow your hand and should not jerk to one side and return. Check that the pupils are equal in size.

3. Face

Ask the diver to whistle. Look carefully to see that both sides of the face have the same expression while whistling. Ask the diver to grit the teeth. Feel the jaw muscles to confirm that they are contracted equally.

Instruct the diver to close the eyes while you lightly touch your fingertips across the forehead and face to be sure sensation is present and the same everywhere.

4. Hearing

Hearing can be evaluated by holding your hand about 60cm from the diver's ear and rubbing your thumb and finger together. Check both ears, moving your hand closer until the diver hears it. Check several times and compare with your own hearing. If the surroundings are noisy, the test is difficult to evaluate. Ask bystanders to be quiet and turn off unneeded machinery.

5. Swallowing Reflex

Instruct the diver to swallow while you watch the "Adam's apple" to be sure it moves up and down.

6. Tongue

Instruct the diver to stick out the tongue. It should come out straight in the middle of the mouth without deviating to either side.

7. Muscle Strength

Instruct the diver to shrug shoulders while you bear down on them to observe for equal muscle strength.

Check diver's arms by bringing the elbows up level with the shoulders, hands level with the arms, and touching the chest. Instruct the diver to resist while you pull the apms away, push them back, up and down. The strength should be approximately equal in both arms in each direction. Check leg strength by having the diver lie flat and raise and lower the legs while you resist the movement.

8. Sensory Perception

Check on both sides by touching lightly as was done on the face. Start at the top of the body and compare sides while moving downwards to cover the entire body. The diver's eyes should be closed during this procedure. The diver should confirm the sensation in each area before you move to another area.

9. Balance and Co-ordination

Be prepared to protect the diver from injury when performing this test. Have the diver stand up with feet together, close eyes and stretch out arms. The diver should be able to maintain balance if the platform is stable. Your arms should be around, but not touching the diver. **Only perform this test on a stable platform and be prepared to catch the diver who starts to fall.**

Check co-ordination by having the diver move an index finger back and forth rapidly between the diver's nose and your finger held approximately 45cm from the diver's face. Instruct the diver to slide the heel of one foot down the shin of the other leg. The diver should be lying down when attempting this test.

Check these tests on both right and left sides and observe carefully for unusual clumsiness on either side.

Tests 1, 7 and 9 are the most important and should be given priority if not all tests can be performed.

The diver's condition may prevent the performance of one or more of these tests. Record any omitted test and the reason. If any of the tests are not normal, injury to the central nervous system should be suspected. The tests should be repeated at frequent intervals while awaiting assistance to determine if any change occurs. Report the results to the emergency medical personnel responding to the call.

Diver's First Aid Kit

All divers should carry an adequate first aid kit and should familiarise themselves with its contents in order to facilitate its correct and rapid use.

We suggest that the following items be included in such a kit:

- A copy of **The Diving Emergency Handbook** and **Oxygen First Aid for Divers**
- **Oxygen** - with appropriate administration equipment
- **Fluids** - for treatment of decompression sickness (2 litres or more of water, electrolyte-type fluids etc.)
- **Vinegar** - large bottle for treating nematocyst stings
- **Local anaesthetic ointment*** - for pain relief from stings
- **Topical antibiotic ointment*, Topical "Betadine"(iodine) paint** or **other antiseptic** - for coral cuts or grazes to prevent or treat infection
- **Ear drops*** - for external ear infections
- **Sea sickness tablets***
- **Analgesics*** - for pain relief (eg. Paracetemol, codene, aspirin)
- **Systemic decongestants*** - for relief from congestion
- **Topical decongestants*** - used as above
- **Eye wash** - to remove foreign body from eyes
- **Three elastic bandages 10cm x 150cm long** - as pressure bandages
- **Pressure bandages/pads** - to control severe bleeding
- **Swabs, crepe bandages, adhesive plaster, "bandaids"**
- **Scissors, tweezers/forceps, sharp knife, needle**
- **Blankets, plastic sheets, sleeping bag**
- **Cold packs** - for pain relief from jellyfish stings
- **Pen and paper** - for recording details of first aid
- **Coins**- for telephone
- **Flashlight**
- **Safety pins** - for securing bandages

*Consult your diving doctor for suitable medications and advice on their use.

Emergency Facilities

HMS Nelson/Gunwharf on Portsmouth: (0705) 818888
DDRC on Plymouth: (0752) 261910 (emergency)

Police:

Ambulance:

Diving Doctors:

Recompression chambers:

Hospitals:

Diving Accident Reporting Organisation:

Use a pencil or permanent overhead transparency pen to fill in the numbers.

Accident Details

This page is designed to be filled out at the scene of a diving accident to ensure that accurate details are given to the treating diving medical specialist. You can write onto the plastic with most pens or pencils.

Name of diver(s):

Details of dive:

- **maximum depth**
- **bottom time**
- **ascent rate (fast, average, slow)**
- **safety stop/decompression stop done**
- **dives in previous 48 hours**

Accident description:

- **location**
- **details**

First Aid given and patient's response:

Further treatment advised:

Diving Emergency Facilities in Various Other Countries

Europe:

Divers Alert Network (DAN) Europe Central Hotline
(c/o REGA Zurich) 41-1-3831111 (this number may change in 1993)

DAN Europe Emergency Operations Headquarters
(c/o ALASERVICE Milano) 39-2-6612766

DAN Europe National Hotlines (with local area codes):

France	IET Toulouse. Call 61-493333.
Germany	German Naval Medical Institute Kiel. Call 0431-54090 and ask for diving doctor on call.
Italy	ALASERVICE Milano. Call 02-6612766.
Malta	Call 09-94193.
Spain	Hyperbaric Unit, Red Cross Hospital, Barcelona. Call 93-4331551 and ask for diving doctor on call.

Australia	DES/DAN Australia. Call 008-088200 from within Australia or call 61-8-2232855 from elsewhere.
Canada	Toronto General Hospital Hyperbaric Unit. Call 416-3404131.
Japan	DAN Japan. 81-3-38124999.
New Zealand	Royal New Zealand Naval Hospital. Call 09-4458454.
South Pacific	Call the Australian or New Zealand emergency number.
USA	The Divers Alert Network (DAN). Call 919-6848111 for emergencies or call 919-6842948 for non-urgent information.

Emergency Communications

DISTRESS SIGNAL
Life threatening emergency

- VHF Channel 16
- Call *MAYDAY MAYDAY MAYDAY*
- Give the name and *position* of your craft
- State the nature of the distress, the number of persons involved and the kind of assistance required
- Give any other information to assist rescue
- If there is no response, repeat the distress call and message, particularly during "silence periods" and also on other frequencies

URGENCY SIGNAL
Medical emergency

- VHF Channel 16
- Call *PANPAN PANPAN PANPAN MEDICO*
- State the name of the local Coastguard
- Call PANPAN MEDICO
- Give the name and *position* of your craft
- State the nature of the distress, the number of persons involved and the kind of assistance required
- Give any other information to assist rescue
- If there is no response, repeat the distress call and message, particularly during "silence periods" and also on other frequencies

Artificial Ventilation

(Administered when patient has a pulse but is not breathing)

Rate: 10 breaths per minute
If regurgitation occurs, roll the patient onto his side, clear his airway, reposition him on his back, ensure adequate head tilt and jaw support and continue Artificial Ventilation, blowing more lightly.
If vomiting occurs, roll the patient onto his side, ensure a clear airway and check for breathing.

The pulse should be checked at approximately one-minute intervals.

Chest Compression

(Administered when patient has no pulse)

Hand position:
Centre of lower half of breastbone

Depth:
4 to 5 cm.

(Gauge spring of breastbone and monitor artificially generated pulse and patient's colour)

Ratio:

1 operator	2 breaths/15 compressions	(approx. 80 compressions
2 operators	1 breath/5 compressions	per minute)

Note 1:
Once Chest Compression has been commenced, it is not necessary to perform further checks for a returned spontaneous pulse.

Note 2:
The rates, positions and depths given above are for an adult patient.